VOLCANO

CHRISTOPHER LAMPTON

THE MILLBROOK PRESS
BROOKFIELD, CT
A DISASTER! BOOK

Cover photograph courtesy of Superstock

Illustrations by Pat Scully

Photographs courtesy of National Geophysical Data Center,
NOAA: pp. 6, 17, 48, 56–57; Superstock: pp. 8–9, 12, 16, 19
(right), 24, 30, 38, 42–43, 45, 52 (both); Art Resource: p.
15; U.S. Geological Survey: pp. 18–19 (J. Rosenbaum), 20
(H.E. Malde); NASA: pp. 40–41.

Cataloging-in-Publication Data

Lampton, Christopher
Volcano / by Christopher Lampton

p. cm.—(A Disaster! Book)
Bibliography p.   Includes index.
Summary: Illustrates four types of volcanoes, explains
what causes eruptions and how lava enriches the soil.
Includes an interesting description of the development
of a volcano.
ISBN 1-56294-028-7   ISBN 0-395-63645-0 (pbk.)
1. Volcanoes. 2. Geology, 3. Earth crust. 4. Mountains.
I. Title. II. Series.
551.2'1   1991

123456789 - WO - 96 95 94 93 92

CONTENTS

22-Jan-97 grant/KMR

THE MOUNTAIN FROM NOWHERE

On February 20, 1943, in the small Mexican village of Parícutin, a farmer named Dionisio Pulido left his house and walked into the fields to tend to his chores, just like he had been doing for years. He knew that there had been an unusual number of earthquakes in the area recently. However, he had no reason to expect to find anything unusual on his farmland.

In the fields, however, he found a crack in the ground with smoke pouring out of it. As he watched, the earth trembled and sparks flew out of the crack and into the air. Some of them settled on the branches of trees and burned the leaves. Within an hour, red-hot lava began to pour out of the crack and onto the surrounding ground. Balls of molten (melted) rock were tossed into the air, pelting the nearby countryside. Clouds of ash billowed upward.

By the next morning, there was a 35-foot-tall mountain in the middle of Dionisio's field—and it was still growing. The mountain was formed out of the lava and ash that had come from the hole in the ground and then cooled in the surrounding air. Within hours, the mountain had more than tripled in size, and by the end of the week

it was a towering 460 feet tall! Needless to say, Dionisio's farm was by then only a memory, buried under the rapidly growing mountain that had sprung unexpectedly from his field.

The mountain in Dionisio's field was a volcano. It spouted ash and dust into the air. Lava poured down its slopes. Eventually, it

Today, a mountain stands in Parícutin where there was nothing only fifty years ago.

grew to be more than 1,000 feet tall. It remained active for nine years, during which time it buried the nearby village of Parícutin in its ash, forcing the evacuation of the villagers. This newborn mountain still stands today in what were once the fields of Dionisio's farm.

VOLCANOES AROUND THE WORLD

There's probably no need to start worrying that a volcano may appear unexpectedly in your neighborhood—or directly under your house. The area around Parícutin was known to be volcanically "active" long before this particular volcano appeared in 1943. There are volcanoes all around the world, but for the most part they are clustered in certain special areas. The Pacific Ocean, for instance, is almost completely surrounded by volcanoes in a circular area known to geologists (scientists who study the earth) as the "Ring of Fire." This "band" of volcanoes is many thousands of miles long and contains hundreds of volcanoes. Most of them, however, have not *erupted*—that is, spewed forth hot lava or other explosive materials—anytime recently.

What are volcanoes? Strictly speaking, they are openings in the earth through which molten rock rises from far below. In many cases, this rock hardens into a mountain surrounding the passageway, or *vent,* through which the hot rock comes to the surface. But not all volcanoes are parts of a mountain. In fact, some volcanoes that have been quiet for many years are hidden below peaceful lakes in the middle of flat or rolling land, not connected with any mountains at all.

However, we usually picture a volcano as a kind of mountain, and some of the most famous mountains in the world are volcanoes, including Mount Fuji in Japan, Mount Vesuvius in Italy, and Mounts Rainier and St. Helens in Washington State. All of these mountains were formed when molten rock came streaming up out of the interior of the earth.

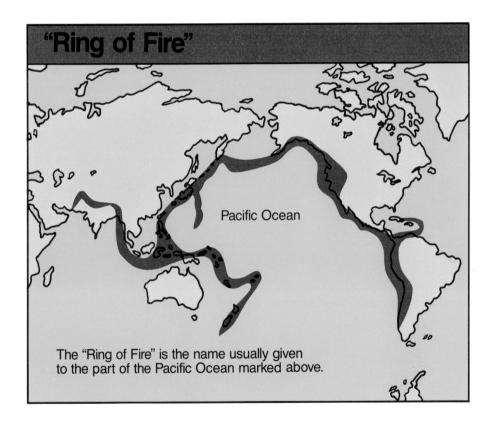

"Ring of Fire"

Pacific Ocean

The "Ring of Fire" is the name usually given to the part of the Pacific Ocean marked above.

Where does the molten rock that rises up in a volcano come from? What makes it rise, often quite violently, to the surface? Those are important questions, and we'll try to answer them, along with other important questions, in the course of this book.

Majestic Mount Rainier in
the state of Washington.

VOLCANOES IN HISTORY

History is filled with stories of volcanoes. Probably the most famous is the eruption of Mount Vesuvius in the year 79 A.D., which buried the nearby Roman cities of Pompeii and Herculaneum under deep piles of lava and ash. The eruption was so sudden that many of the people living in these towns failed to evacuate in time and found themselves trapped in their homes by the heavy rain of ash pouring from the sky. The people in the cities died from the poisonous gases and suffocation in the ash cloud. Then, even as Pompeii was being buried under 20 feet of ash, Herculaneum disappeared under a mudslide triggered by the eruption.

More than 1,500 years later, archaeologists rediscovered these cities where they lay buried. Amazingly, the mud and ash had formed solid casts around the long-ago decayed bodies of the victims. By filling these casts with plaster, the archaeologists were able to create statues of the citizens of Pompeii and Herculaneum, some fleeing in terror and others simply carrying on with their daily lives, totally

*An artist's depiction of the eruption
at Mount Vesuvius in 79 A.D.*

Solid casts of Vesuvius's victims in the city of Pompeii were found 1,500 years after the eruption. From these molds scientists made plaster casts that are now on exhibit for all to see.

unaware of the disaster about to strike. Many items from ancient Roman society were preserved in nearly perfect condition. The rediscovery of these two cities, destroyed long ago by a volcanic eruption, was one of the greatest archaeological finds of all time.

Almost as famous was the eruption of Krakatau (also known as Krakatoa) in the Indian Ocean in 1883. This volcanic island near Java spewed out ash and lava several times over a period of a few days, climaxing in one of the most violent volcanic eruptions of modern times. So loud was the eruption that it was heard in Australia, almost 2,000 miles away. The force of the eruption created a giant wave that killed 30,000 people on Krakatau and neighboring islands. The only known surviving witnesses to the explosion were in a pair of ships that had become trapped in the ash clouds, unable to navigate away from the island.

On May 8, 1902, the Mount Pelée volcano on the island of Saint-Pierre in the West Indies erupted, triggering an avalanche of hot materials that swept across the town. It killed all but two of the island's 28,000 inhabitants. One of the survivors was a prisoner who was being held in an underground dungeon at the time of the eruption.

In 1980, the most famous volcano in the United States, Mount St. Helens near Seattle, Washington, burst forth with an eruption that had been anticipated by scientists for some months. An entire side of the mountain collapsed under the force of the explosion, releasing a cloud of ash that traveled many miles from the volcano. The explosion killed 57 people and caused more than $1 billion worth of damage. A small plane carrying a pair of *volcanologists*— scientists who study volcanoes—was circling the mountain at the time and was nearly caught in the explosion.

The volcano at Mount St. Helens in the state of Washington blew up in a massive explosion in 1980.

The explosion caused great devastation to trees and other vegetation in the area of Mount St. Helens.

A VOLCANO
CHRONICLE

Here's a quick look at some of the other major volcanic eruptions from the past two hundred years:

■ 1986: An eruption of gas from an ancient volcanic lake spread a cloud of poisonous carbon dioxide over an area of approximately 6 square miles, killing more than 1,500 people in Cameroon, West Africa.

■ 1985: Mudflows on the slope of the Nevado del Ruiz volcano in Colombia buried much of the town of Armero, killing 23,000 people.

■ 1982: Erupting three times in one week, the El Chichon volcano in Mexico released half a billion tons of ash into the earth's atmosphere, devastating a wide area and killing several people. That same year, the Galunggung volcano in Indonesia burst to life for the first time in more than a century and a half, burying several villages under deep drifts of ash. Fortunately, the area had been evacuated at the first sign of an eruption. Few people were killed.

■ 1977: After smoldering for decades, the Nyirangongo volcano in Zaire, Africa, came back to life with a vengeance, pouring lava onto nearby villages and killing 1,200 people.

■ 1968: Mt. Arenal in Costa Rica propelled blocks of lava for miles around and killed 80 people with several landslides on its slopes.

■ 1956: In a spectacular eruption that fortunately claimed no lives, the Bezymianny volcano rained hot ash down on a 200-square-mile area in Kamchatka, USSR.

■ 1952: A brand-new volcanic island appeared off the coast of Japan, then disappeared again into the sea. A total of 31 men died while investigating the volcano from a submarine just as the volcano erupted.

■ 1951: The sound from the explosion of Mt. Lamington in New Guinea echoed 200 miles away as a glowing cloud of hot dust killed 3,000 people in a 90-square-mile area around the volcano.

■ 1919: Mud from the Kelut volcano in Indonesia buried 104 villages, killing 5,000 people.

■ 1911: After the eruption of the Taal volcano in the Philippines, the cloud of ash that settled back to earth killed more than 1,000 people.

■ 1897: Although it erupted 26 times in one century, this eruption of the Mayon volcano in the Philippines was the worst. An entire town was destroyed and hundreds of people were killed, some as far as 100 miles from the eruption.

■ 1888: Four villages were buried under an avalanche when the Bandai-San volcano in Japan erupted, killing 500 people.

■ 1835: Although it killed no one (as far as anybody knows), the eruption of Cosequina in Nicaragua was one of the largest volcanic eruptions of recent centuries. Debris rained down on cities more than 100 miles away, and the area around the volcano was thrown into a darkness as black as night. The sound of the eruption was heard as far away as Jamaica.

■ 1822: The Galunggung volcano in Indonesia, which would erupt again in 1982, killed 4,000 people in a massive eruption.

■ 1815: The Tambora volcano in Indonesia blew away much of its surrounding mountain in an explosion heard more than 1,000 miles away.

MAGMA FROM THE DEPTHS

The surface of the earth is usually a peaceful place, which is why we think of volcanoes as unusual. Hot lava doesn't ordinarily come spewing out of the ground. But the interior of the earth is quite a different place. If you were to plunge 50 or 60 miles beneath the earth's surface, you would find yourself in much hotter surroundings, where hot rock and blistering temperatures are commonplace. This is where the molten lava that powers volcanoes comes from.

Why is the earth so hot inside? The earth formed about four and a half billion years ago from the collision of millions of small rocky particles that were in orbit together around the sun. The friction of these collisions heated the planet until it was almost molten. Most of that heat escaped into space long ago. However, the earth's interior has been kept hot by the breakdown of radioactive elements inside the planet. These are the same sorts of elements that power the steam engines inside a nuclear power plant. In fact, the interior of the earth can be looked at as a kind of giant nuclear power plant.

Fortunately for human beings, the surface of our hot planet is covered with a cool, hard, rocky layer known as the *crust.* The crust

*Here is a rare glimpse into the hot liquid heart
of a volcano, the Kilauea volcano in Hawaii.*

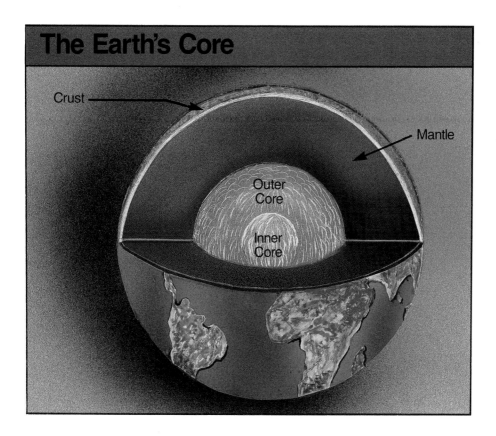

The Earth's Core

Crust

Mantle

Outer Core

Inner Core

extends all over the surface of the earth, even below the oceans. But the crust is only a few dozen miles thick. Under the crust is the hot, semi-liquid *mantle,* on which the crust floats like a raft in water.

The crust is solid, but it is not all one piece. It is broken up into fifteen major pieces (with many smaller fragments), called *plates.* Each of these plates floats on the mantle independently of the others. All of them are in motion, pushed or pulled along by the heat of the earth's interior.

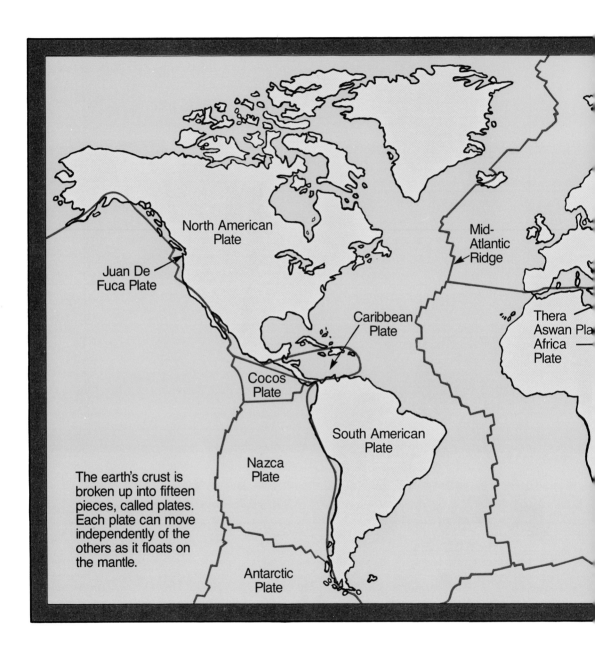

North American
Plate

Juan De
Fuca Plate

Mid-
Atlantic
Ridge

Caribbean
Plate

Thera
Aswan Pla
Africa
Plate

Cocos
Plate

South American
Plate

The earth's crust is
broken up into fifteen
pieces, called plates.
Each plate can move
independently of the
others as it floats on
the mantle.

Nazca
Plate

Antarctic
Plate

The Earth's Plates

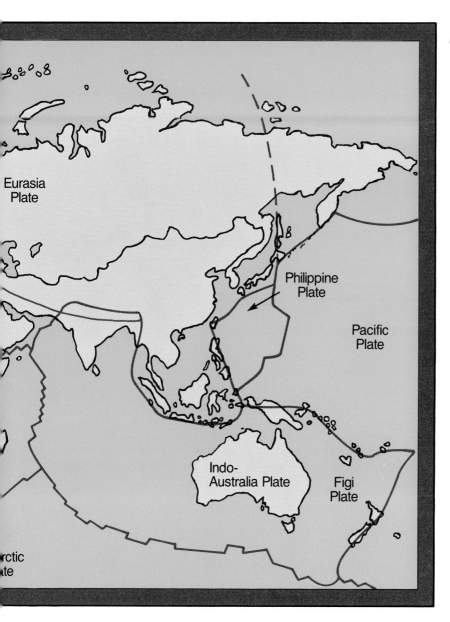

Eurasia Plate

Philippine Plate

Pacific Plate

Indo-Australia Plate

Figi Plate

rctic te

Because these plates are crowded tightly onto the surface of the earth, you might wonder just where they can move *to.* In some cases, they are moving apart. But if some plates are moving apart, then other plates must be moving together. And, indeed, this is the case.

The region where two plates are moving apart is called a *rift zone,* because a rift, or rip, in the earth's crust opens between the two plates. Most rift zones are at the bottom of the ocean. One of the largest rift zones is found in the middle of the Atlantic Ocean, far beneath the surface of the waves. Several plates are moving apart from one another at this rift, including the North American plate (which lies under most of the North American continent) and the Eurasian plate (which lies under Europe and much of Asia). As these plates move apart, hot molten rock from inside the earth rises up through the rift to the surface.

Hot rock deep beneath the earth is called *magma,* but when it reaches the surface we call it *lava.* The Mid-Atlantic Rift probably has more active volcanoes than any other area on earth. But we never see these volcanoes because they are at the bottom of the ocean. The mountains that form around these volcanoes make up the largest mountain range on earth, far beneath the surface of the sea. The only part of this range that rises above the water's surface is the island nation of Iceland, which is dotted with both inactive and active volcanoes.

As the magma inside these undersea volcanoes rises up from the depths, it gradually cools and becomes part of the seafloor. In this way, new seafloor is constantly being created in the middle of the ocean. For this reason, the rift itself never gets larger, even as the plates move farther and farther apart. Since the plates that include the continents of North and South America and the plates that

The Mid-Atlantic Rift Zone

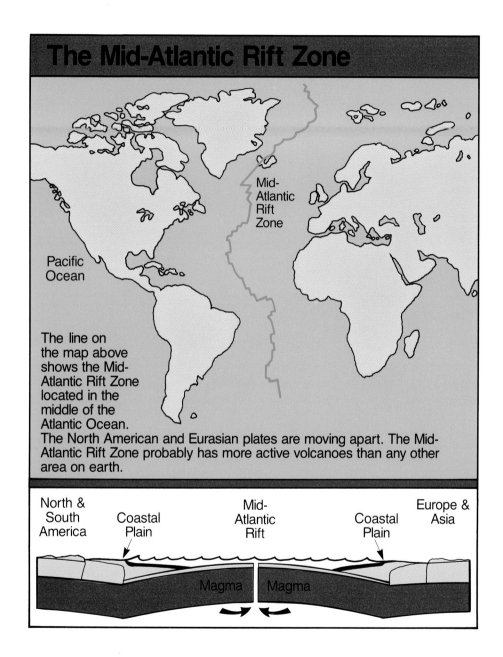

Mid-
Atlantic
Rift
Zone

Pacific
Ocean

The line on the map above shows the Mid-Atlantic Rift Zone located in the middle of the Atlantic Ocean.

The North American and Eurasian plates are moving apart. The Mid-Atlantic Rift Zone probably has more active volcanoes than any other area on earth.

North &
South
America

Coastal
Plain

Mid-
Atlantic
Rift

Coastal
Plain

Europe &
Asia

Magma   Magma

include the continents of Europe and Africa are moving apart, these continents are also moving apart. Millions of years ago, these continents were joined together to form a single "supercontinent" that geologists call *Pangaea* (pan-GEE-uh), from Greek words meaning "all the world."

*Iceland is dotted with
active volcanoes.*

SUBDUCTION ZONES

The volcanoes of the Mid-Atlantic Rift are created when hot magma flows up through the rift from the interior of the earth. But where do the volcanoes that are not part of the rift come from? Most of them occur at *subduction zones,* places where the edges of two plates are coming together.

When two plates collide, one plate usually rides up over the top of the other. The lower plate is forced down into the mantle, the hot semi-liquid layer beneath the crust. As the lower plate descends into the earth, it gets hotter, until it begins to melt. The lighter elements in the crust then rise back up through the mantle, like bubbles rising in carbonated soda. Eventually, this hot, molten rock comes up from beneath the overriding plate. It seeps through cracks in the crust until it reaches the surface and becomes lava. And sometimes the magma may actually melt its way through the crust, forming brand-new cracks.

Once the magma gets to the surface and becomes lava, a volcano is born. (If there is already a volcano where the hot rock reaches the surface, that volcano comes back to life.)

All of the volcanoes around the Ring of Fire were formed in this way. The volcanoes in Washington State and Oregon, for instance, are located above a subduction zone where the Juan de Fuca plate (a small plate in the northeastern Pacific Ocean) is subducted under the North American plate. On the other side of the Pacific, many volcanoes occur where the Pacific plate is subducted under the Philippine and Eurasian plates.

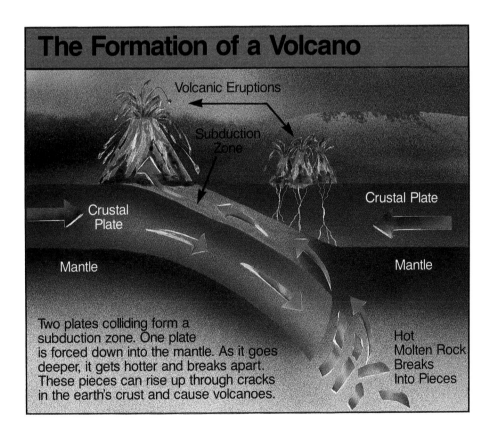

The Formation of a Volcano

Volcanic Eruptions

Subduction Zone

Crustal Plate

Crustal Plate

Mantle

Mantle

Two plates colliding form a subduction zone. One plate is forced down into the mantle. As it goes deeper, it gets hotter and breaks apart. These pieces can rise up through cracks in the earth's crust and cause volcanoes.

Hot Molten Rock Breaks Into Pieces

HOT
SPOTS

But not all volcanoes are located at the edges of plates. The island of Hawaii, for instance, is famous for its active volcanoes. Yet it's right in the middle of the Pacific plate.

Volcanologists aren't absolutely sure why Hawaii has volcanoes, but the most popular theory says that Hawaii is located directly above a *hot spot* in the earth's crust. A hot spot is a place somewhere underneath the crust where an unusual amount of hot magma is being produced.

What makes hot spots so hot? Scientists are not sure. Maybe hot spots contain an unusually large amount of the radioactive elements that produce heat inside the earth. Whatever the reason, the magma in a hot spot apparently melts its way through the overlying plate. It bubbles to the surface to form a volcano.

The plates that make up the crust, however, are moving, so a hot spot doesn't affect the same place for long. If you look at a map of the Pacific, you'll see that the island of Hawaii is at the end of a long chain of islands beginning in the northwest with the island of

Midway and ending in the southeast with Hawaii. Each of these islands is volcanic in origin—that is, the islands were formed out of volcanic lava rising up through a vent in the crust beneath the ocean.

If a single hot spot created these islands, it would seem to be moving southeastward across the Pacific plate. But the hot spot itself isn't actually moving. It is the Pacific plate that is moving northwestward, while the hot spot apparently stays in the same place.

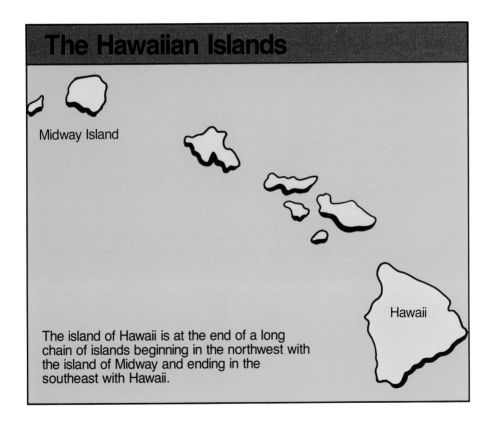

The Hawaiian Islands

Midway Island

Hawaii

The island of Hawaii is at the end of a long chain of islands beginning in the northwest with the island of Midway and ending in the southeast with Hawaii.

Geologists studying the rocks on the islands found that those on the southeast end of the chain are newer than those on the northwest end. The rocks on the island of Hawaii, for instance, are less than a million years old. The rocks on Oahu, to the northwest of Hawaii, are two to three million years old. To the southeast of Hawaii, on the other hand, there is a relatively recent underwater volcano that will probably rise up out of the sea one day to become a new island in the chain.

There are more than 40 hot spots around the world. There may be a hot spot in the Mid-Atlantic Rift itself, under the island of Iceland. The extra volcanic activity provided by this hot spot would explain why Iceland is the only part of the mountain range along the rift that rises above the surface of the water.

MANY KINDS OF VOLCANOES

There are many different kinds of volcanoes. There are also many different kinds of volcanic eruptions.

One classification used by volcanologists refers to the volcano's level of activity. Depending on when it last erupted, a volcano can be classified as *active, dormant,* or *extinct.*

Some authorities define an active volcano as one that has erupted within the last fifty years. A dormant volcano is one for which there is an historical record of an eruption, but that eruption did not take place within the last fifty years. An extinct volcano is one for which there is no historical record of an eruption. Unfortunately, this doesn't tell us much about what these volcanoes are going to do in the future. A volcano for which there is no historical record of an eruption may suddenly explode back to life tomorrow. A dormant volcano can wake up just as suddenly.

Other classifications of volcanoes are based on the physical structures that have been formed around them by cooling lava. A *shield volcano,* for instance, doesn't really look the way we normally

expect volcanoes to look. Instead of a steep mountain, a shield volcano is surrounded by gently sloped hills in a circular or fan-shaped pattern (though these hills can still rise to an impressive height). It is named for its resemblance, when seen from above, to the heraldic shields carried by the knights of long ago. Shield volcanoes form when lava flows gently and continuously out of the volcanic vent, gradually accumulating and cooling around the volcano.

The Kilauea volcano on the island of Hawaii is a shield volcano. At the moment, Kilauea is one of the most active volcanoes on earth. It erupted repeatedly throughout the 1980s and shows no sign of quieting down anytime soon. Fortunately, Kilauea's eruptions present no threat to the island's inhabitants, though its lava has burned down dozens of houses near the volcano. (The inhabitants of these houses were evacuated before they could be harmed.)

Volcanoes are not restricted to our planet. Perhaps the most impressive of all known shield volcanoes is on Mars. Given the name *Olympus Mons* ("Mount Olympus"), it was discovered by a space probe orbiting Mars and sending pictures back to earth.

Olympus Mons is an extinct volcano, as are the other volcanoes that have been observed on Mars. But Io, one of the moons of Jupiter, features several currently active volcanoes. So does Triton, one of the moons of Neptune. But the volcanoes on Triton are very different from those on earth. They erupt nitrogen heated by the light of the distant sun.

Lava flowing down the mountainside at Kilauea.

Volcanoes can exist on worlds other than our own. Shown are volcanoes on Jupiter's moon Io (above) and the Martian volcano Olympus Mons (right).

Stratovolcanoes, also known as composite volcanoes, are probably closer to what you picture in your mind when you hear the word "volcano." They are tall, cone-shaped mountains made out of lava, ash, and fragments of a type of composite rock known as pyroclastic.

Mount Fuji, a composite volcano, is one of the most painted sites in the world.

Mount Fuji in Japan is a composite volcano. (Regarded as one of the most beautiful mountains in the world, Mount Fuji has probably appeared in more paintings than any other mountain anywhere.) Many other well-known volcanoes, such as Mount St. Helens and Mount Vesuvius, are also composite volcanoes.

This spectacular cinder-cone volcano erupted in Nicaragua in 1971.

Cinder-cone volcanoes are smaller and simpler than composite volcanoes. The lava erupting from the volcano forms into tiny cinderlike rocks as it flies through the air. These rocks form a cone-shaped pile around the volcano.

A fully formed volcano can collapse to form a *caldera*. Calderas are huge pits in the ground surrounded by steep walls. The calderas of inactive volcanoes often fill with water and become lakes. Crater Lake in Oregon, for instance, is the caldera of an inactive volcano.

Crater Lake in Oregon.

Sometimes a structure known as a *magma* (or *lava*) *dome* (also called a *neck*) will form in the vent of a composite volcano. Made out of hardened lava, the dome is pressed upward by the force of fresh magma from below. Such domes can grow for days on end. The volcanic pressures trapped beneath a magma dome can be released suddenly to produce a major eruption, such as the eruptions of Mount Pelée in 1902 and Mount St. Helens in 1980.

Although they are not precisely volcanoes, *geysers* such as those in Yellowstone National Park are also created by hot spots in the earth's mantle. A geyser occurs when underground water comes into contact with hot rocks beneath the earth and returns to the surface in the form of steam and boiling water. Sometimes only steam makes it back to the surface, creating a *fumarole. Hot springs* are also caused by the underground heating of water.

TYPES OF ERUPTIONS

Volcanologists also divide the eruptions of volcanoes into different types. The same volcano can produce more than one type of eruption.

The *Strombolian* type of eruption, for instance, is named after a volcano on the island of Stromboli in Italy. In Strombolian eruptions, hot gases trapped inside the volcano periodically burst loose to send lava and rocks splattering out of the volcano. Such an eruption can continue for years on end.

Phreatic eruptions are explosions of steam. They occur when groundwater comes into contact with hot rock inside a volcano. As the water changes rapidly to steam, it bursts through the rock layers, creating a violent explosion.

Plinian eruptions are named for the Roman historian Pliny the Elder, who was killed in the eruption of Mount Vesuvius in 79 A.D. Shortly before his death, Pliny commented that the plume of smoke rising above the volcano resembled a pine tree. (Today it might remind us more of the mushroom cloud created by a nuclear explosion.) In a Plinian eruption, lava clogging the vent of the volcano is

A Plinian eruption is shaped like the
mushroom cloud from a nuclear explosion.

blown out of the way by the force of the rising magma. Volcanic particles thrust high above the volcano take on the pine-tree shape noted by Pliny.

In a *Hawaiian-type eruption,* lava flows freely out of the volcano, with few violent explosions. In *underwater* (or *submarine*) *eruptions,* the lava cools rapidly on contact with the water and builds up around the volcano in piles called *pillow lava.* A *nuee ardente* (or *Pelean*) *eruption* involves a landslide of hot, glowing materials that flows down the side of the volcano overwhelming everything in its path. The eruption of Mount Pelée in 1902 involved a *nuee ardente.* (*Nuee ardente* is a French expression meaning "burning"— or "glowing"—"cloud."

VOLCANIC ROCK

Most of the rocks that make up the earth's crust were originally created by the heat and pressure inside volcanoes. However, over thousands, millions, or even billions of years, this rock has changed form. Erosion—from wind, rain, and the roots of growing plants—has ground it into dirt and gravel. Many of these fragments of rock have been swept up by the water in rivers and streams, eventually to be dumped on the ocean bottom where they formed *sedimentary rock.*

Some rocks, however, are still in their original volcanic forms. This is especially true in regions of active and dormant volcanoes. Different types of volcanic rocks take different forms. Because these have different chemical contents, they are given different names.

Dark black volcanic rocks, for instance, are called *basalt lava* and are poor in silica, the material from which glass and ceramics are made. Reddish or light-colored volcanic rocks, known as *rhyolite,* are much richer in silica.

Large, boulderlike chunks of cooled lava are known as *bombs,* because they often shoot into the air during a volcanic eruption and

These basalt boulders are located on the right bank of the Snake River near Bancroft Springs in Idaho.

51

Pahoehoe formed from lava from the Kilauea volcano in Hawaii.

The interior of Split Mountain, located near Flagstaff, Arizona, exposes the pumice walls of an extinct volcano.

come crashing to the ground. Pieces of larger volcanic rocks, broken off during an eruption, are called *blocks.* Smaller pieces of lava are called *dust* or *ash.*

In Hawaii, there are large fields of hardened lava known as *Pahoehoe* (pronounced "pah-HOY-hoy") and *aa* ("ah-ah"). The first type is made of relatively smooth, ropelike strands. The second is blocky and jagged, so full of sharp edges that it would slice your feet to ribbons if you walked on it barefoot. (Even boots have a short lifetime on *aa,* which is supposedly named for the sounds of pain made by a person who accidentally stumbles onto a bed of it.)

One of the most spectacular volcanic remains is called *Pele's hair,* because it is arranged in glassy strands. *Pumice* is a spongy form of volcanic rock, full of holes. In some cases, it can actually float on water.

BENEFITS FROM VOLCANOES

Volcanic eruptions cause billions of dollars in damage and have taken thousands of lives. It would seem that no good could come of a volcano. Yet this isn't so. Volcanoes are part of natural geologic processes that made our world what it is today. They can enrich the planet as well as damage it.

The very atmosphere of earth today, in fact, originally came from volcanoes. The earth's early atmosphere was blown away by a "wind" of energetic particles from the sun. Our planet would be barren and airless today if it weren't for volcanoes releasing gases from the earth's interior to create a second atmosphere. Of course, this volcanic atmosphere would not be breathable by human beings if it were not for the plants that came along billions of years later and converted the carbon dioxide in this atmosphere into oxygen.

Volcanic ash is a surprisingly good fertilizer. Supposedly, there are tribes in New Guinea that perform volcano dances, the way that some American Indian tribes once performed rain dances.

Diamonds and other gems that form far beneath the ground are brought to the surface by volcanic activity. Many diamond mines have been found in regions of extinct volcanoes.

PREDICTING VOLCANOES

If we are going to save the lives of people who would otherwise be killed in volcanic eruptions, we will have to predict those eruptions in advance. And, in fact, volcanoes usually send out warning signals before they erupt. Earthquake tremors (that is, a shaking of the ground) frequently occur as magma works its way through underground vents to the surface.

However, not all volcanic eruptions are dangerous. Only three out of one hundred pose a threat to those living nearby.

Volcanologists realize that if they predict a volcanic eruption that doesn't happen, or that isn't deadly enough to worry about, the public may not trust predictions that they make in the future. Predictions of a volcanic eruption can't be made lightly. Evacuating the area around a volcano can be expensive and disruptive, and reports of dangerous volcanic activity can cause serious economic hardship to areas that depend on tourism.

Many instruments have been developed to monitor the behavior of volcanoes. Seismometers can detect even the tiniest of earthquake tremors. And special instruments placed on the volcano itself can detect the shifting of the magma inside the vent.

Still, it is difficult to tell when signs of volcanic activity mean that public warnings of danger should be issued. As volcanologists study volcanoes, however, they are becoming more knowledgeable

This composite volcano in Guatemala has erupted over twenty-two times since its birth in 1565—and almost every year since 1965. Not all volcanoes follow such predictable behavior, however.

about the signals that foretell dangerous volcanic activity. Someday they may be able to make accurate predictions that can save thousands of lives in the event of a volcanic eruption.

GLOSSARY

aa—fields of cracked and jagged hardened lava, commonly found in Hawaii; pronounced "ah-ah," supposedly the sound someone makes when walking on it with bare feet.

active—describes a volcano that has erupted within approximately the last fifty years.

ash—small fragments of lava.

basalt lava—dark volcanic rocks that are poor in silica.

blocks—broken-off pieces of larger volcanic rocks.

bombs—large boulderlike chunks of cooled lava that shoot out of a volcano during an eruption.

caldera—a pit in the ground left by a collapsed volcano.

cinder-cone volcano—a smaller, simpler version of a composite volcano; a volcano surrounded by a small cone of volcanic rock.

composite volcano—see stratovolcano.

crust—the outermost layer of the planet earth; a rocky layer floating on top of the semi-liquid mantle below.

dormant—describes a volcano that is known to have erupted in historical times.

dust—small pieces of lava.

extinct—describes a volcano that has not erupted in historical times.

fumarole—a burst of steam that occurs when underground water comes in contact with hot molten rock.

geyser—an "eruption" of hot water that occurs when underground water comes in contact with hot molten rock.

Hawaiian-type eruption—a gentle volcanic eruption in which lava flows freely out of the volcano with few violent explosions.

hot spot—a location beneath the earth's crust where the molten rock in the mantle is unusually hot, perhaps because of an excess of radioactive materials.

hot springs—pools of water warmed by hot rock beneath the ground.

lava—hot molten rock from the earth's mantle that has come to the surface through a vent in the earth's crust.

lava dome—a barrier of hardened lava that forms in the vent of a volcano, allowing volcanic pressure to become trapped inside the vent until it bursts loose in a powerful eruption.

magma—the molten rocky material that makes up the earth's mantle, maintained in a semi-liquid state by the pressure of the heavy crust above.

mantle—the semi-liquid layer directly below the earth's outer crust.

nuee ardente—a volcanic eruption accompanied by a landslide of hot, glowing materials down the side of the volcano; from a French phrase meaning "burning cloud."

Pahoehoe—fields of hardened lava in smooth, ropelike strands commonly found in Hawaii; pronounced "pah-HOY-hoy."

Pangaea—pronounced "pan-GEE-uh," the supercontinent that existed on earth millions of years ago when all of the major landmasses of the earth's crust had come together to form a single landmass.

Pele's hair—glassy strands of hardened volcanic material.

phreatic eruption—steam explosions that occur when groundwater comes into contact with hot rock inside a volcano.

pillow lava—piles of hardened lava surrounding an underwater volcanic eruption.

plates—the independently moving pieces of the earth's crust.

·*Plinian eruptions*—a volcanic eruption in which lava clogging the vent of the volcano is blown out of the way by the force of the rising magma.

pumice—a spongy form of volcanic rock, full of holes.

pyroclastic rock—a type of rock made out of volcanic fragments.

rhyolite—light, reddish-colored volcanic rocks, rich in silica.

rift zone—the region in which two of the plates that make up the earth's crust are moving apart from one another, leaving a gap, or rift, in the crust.

sedimentary rock—rock formed from materials deposited at the bottom of a body of water.

shield volcano—a volcano surrounded by gently sloping hills in a circular or fan-shaped pattern.

stratovolcano—a volcano surrounded by a tall, cone-shaped mountain made out of lava, ash, and pyroclastic rock; also known as a composite volcano.

Strombolian eruption—a volcanic eruption in which hot gases trapped inside the volcano periodically send lava and rocks spewing into the air.

underwater eruption—an underwater volcanic eruption in which lava cools on contact with the water and builds up around the volcano in hardened piles.

vent—an opening in the earth's crust through which molten rock can pour from the hot mantle below.

RECOMMENDED READING

Kiefer, Irene. *Global Jigsaw Puzzle: The Story of Continental Drift.* New York: Atheneum, 1980.

Lambert, David. *Volcanoes.* New York: Franklin Watts, 1985.

Lauber, Patricia. *The Eruption and Healing of Mt. St. Helens.* New York: Bradbury Press, 1988.

Rutland, Jonathan. *Exploring the Violent Earth.* New York: Warwick Press, 1980.

Simon, Seymour. *Volcanoes.* New York: Morrow, 1988.

Vogt, Gregory. *Predicting Volcanic Eruptions.* New York: Franklin Watts, 1989.

INDEX